6/93

Modern Design in Wood

By Richard Stewart
Modern Design in Metal

Modern Design in Wood

Richard Stewart

John Murray · London

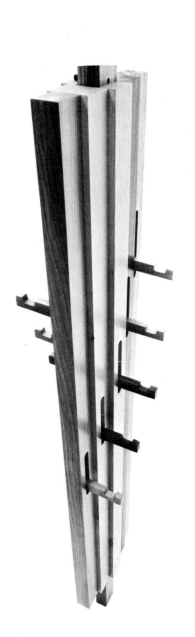

Contents

Printed in Great Britain by J. W. Arrowsmith Ltd,
Bristol BS3 2NT

0 7195 3536 0

Acknowledgments

The author is indebted to the designers, manufacturers and photographers, both in this country and abroad, who have generously provided illustrations and information for inclusion in this volume, and in particular the following organisations:

   Abitare Magazine, Italy
   The Arts Council of Great Britain
   The Design Council
   The Crafts Advisory Committee
   The Finnish Foreign Trade Association
   Jane Gate Photographs
   Willi Müller, Switzerland
   Office Suisse d'Expansion Commerciale
   The Society of Industrial Artists and Designers
   The Tate Gallery
   Adrian Webster Agencies

Introduction

With the growing emphasis on design education and consumer discrimination it is hoped that this new selection of annotated photographs will satisfy the need for a stimulating and up-to-date source of reference in the woodworking field.

Despite man's increased exploitation of synthetic materials, wood remains a favourite constructional and expressive medium suited to both mass production techniques and to individual work in the school or home. For the craftsman, great satisfaction lies in the use of well-tried tools and processes perfected over centuries of use. At the same time, the introduction of plywood, chipboard and blockboard has freed design from the domination of the framed and panelled unit. In addition versatile power tools and improved adhesives, finishes and fittings help ensure success in the creation of attractive and functional products for the modern home.

The chosen illustrations demonstrate the continued ability of designers to produce original solutions to fundamental problems such as seating and storage. Included are examples from this country and abroad, particularly Italy with its flair for design and Scandinavia with its knowledge and respect for the material.

Many of the products illustrated have been selected by the Design Council for their Index, having satisfied criteria of functional and visual excellence. Some are award-winning designs and others already have become modern classics, created by now famous names working in the best traditions of twentieth-century functionalism. Both one-off commissions and mass-produced articles skilfully exploit the potential of the medium to optimum effect. For reference purposes the collection of some 200 illustrations has been grouped into seven chapters. Designs range from simpler products with an aesthetic or recreational content through to larger more functional articles of furniture, and the following points of interest are brought to the reader's attention:

Sculpture and Jewellery

The warmth and texture of wood make it ideal for carving natural forms where the grain helps define and inspire the contours. At school level competent results can be produced with Surform tools which are safe for younger pupils to use, while offcuts and veneers can be utilised in basic jewellery exercises at little cost.

Woodware

Numerous small artefacts traditionally made from wood are now being moulded in plastic. Nevertheless hardwood containers of all kinds retain their appeal, being attractive possessions in their own right as well as enhancing their contents. Similarly, trays, bowls and condiment sets in teak and other woods are popular and perfectly functional when appropriately sealed and finished.

Toys and Recreational Equipment

Play is a fundamental activity for the young and many professional designers have turned to creating toys which are both educational and recreational. In school workshops the making of toys – whether for pupils or their younger relations and friends – is excellent project work. Wood, preferably beech which is free of smells and is non-toxic, is more attractive to handle and stronger than plastic.

Stools, Chairs and Settees

Essentially a means of supporting the human form seventeen inches or so from the ground, the chair has received perhaps more attention than any other article of furniture. Under Scandinavian influence the traditional rectilinear structure has been refined to an elegant simplicity in rose-wood or teak. Also partly pioneered in Scandinavia, laminated frames and moulded plywood seats enable the cantilever designs of metal furniture to be equalled. More recently, knock-down or quick-assembly constructions with screw fittings and alloy joints have reduced the reliance on mortice and tenon joints.

Tables and Dining Suites

Man-made boards richly veneered with rosewood, walnut and teak create stable, flat tops for frames of solid wood or chromed steel of knock-down construction – necessary features for delivery, perhaps using the family car, to a high rise, centrally heated flat. Growing in popularity are refectory tables and benches in solid, even veneered, pine for kitchen/dining areas. Hard Polyurethane varnish, available in matt or semi-matt finishes, helps protect delicate veneers or softwoods.

Cabinets, Desks and Sideboards

Some of the most elegant designs have been created by contract furnishers for the rationalised office or executive suite, combining expensive veneers with chrome, glass and stainless steel. The long, low sideboard is still popular and may be fitted with dismountable bookcase units, although more specialist cabinets for drinks, records and hi-fi are tending to replace it.

Modular and Fitted Furniture

Modular systems with their standardised measurements and limited number of components have led to major changes in furniture design. They usually exploit man-made boards, laminates and ingenious fittings which can be assembled to suit, and indeed define, the size and function of an area whether for recreation, rest or study. Furthermore, even quite modest kitchens are able to boast a range of interchangeable work and storage units, and systems are becoming available for the bathroom. Hopefully, a majority of late twentieth-century interiors will have a harmonious pattern of modular units uncluttered by free-standing cupboards, sideboards and cabinets.

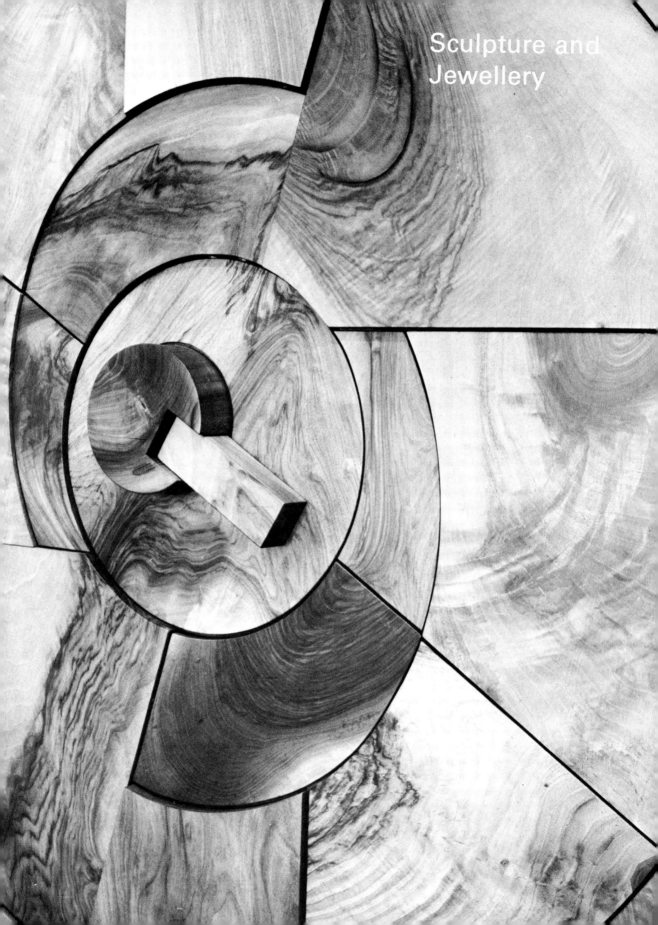

Sculpture and
Jewellery

Four sculptures by Barbara Hepworth inspired by local environment and natural form.

'HOLLOW FORM WITH WHITE'
Elm

◁ **DECORATIVE PANEL**
Part of a cabinet door exploiting the grain of solid walnut.

For details see page 74

'FORMS IN ECHELON'
Tulipwood

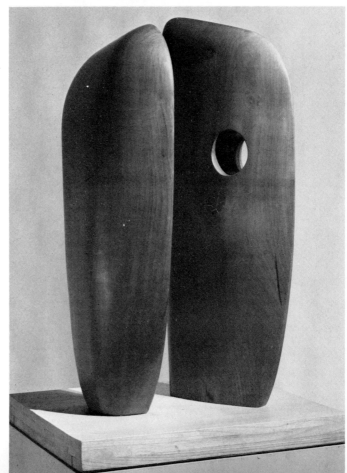

2

'TIDES 1'
Holly

'PELAGOS'
Elm with coloured
string

3

'STANDING FIGURE'
Carved from a large
block of elm.
Sculptor: Bernard
Meadows

'FIGURE'
Carved from several
layers of multiply.
Sculptor: Geoffrey
O'Connell

'SEA FORM'
Oiled teak.
Sculptor: Michael Day

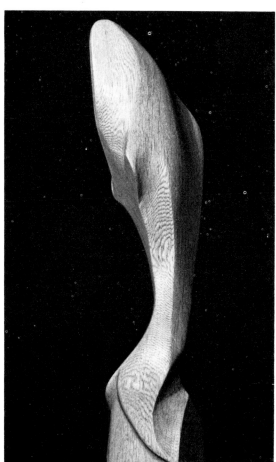

'LEAPING FISH'
Japanese oak.
Sculptor: Mike Smith

A selection of jewellery exercises exploiting contrasting woods and shapes.

PENDANT

Strips of birch and mahogany cut to 45° after lamination.

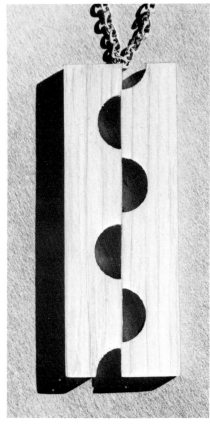

PENDANT

The strip of pine was bored with holes, cut along the centre line and the two halves repositioned.

HAIR SLIDE

Veneers of rosewood and birch laminated in a curved hardwood former.

PENDANT
Veneers of rosewood
and birch.

WOGGLES
Beech rings bored with
Forstner bits and
inserted with birch and
mahogany dowels
formed by plug cutters.
Made by Ralph Furze

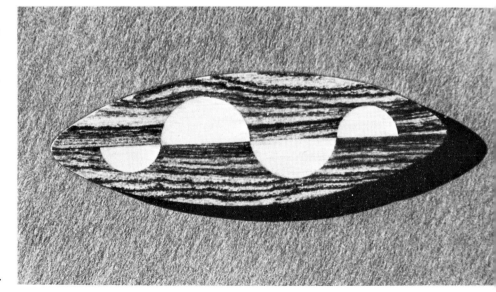

BROOCH
Ebony with birch plugs.

'WHITE WOOD RELIEF'
Limewood on ply.
Sculptor: Sergio de Camargo

'WHITE FACED RELIEF'
Painted wood.
Sculptor: Mary Martin

Woodware

CLOCKS

Teak boxes house the electrical movements. The three dials are turned from one piece of teak on a face-plate.

Designed by J. P. Byrne and made by Timecraft, Liverpool

CLOCK

Pine case with inlaid plastic markings. Battery-operated electronic movement.

Designed and made by George Sneed

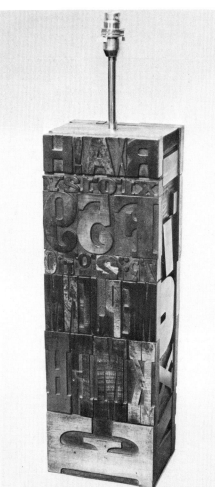

◁ BOXES

Turned from Huon pine.

Designed and made by Richard Raffan

TABLE LAMP

Carefully arranged printing blocks.

Designed and made by Brian Bradley

LIGHT SHADE

Strips of pine, all the same length.

Designed by Colin Cooper and made by Hamlet Furniture Ltd

COAT HANGER

Contrasting woods with pull-down hooks and telescopic application from floor to ceiling.

Designed by Pompeo Pianezzola and made by Appiani Selezione (Italy)

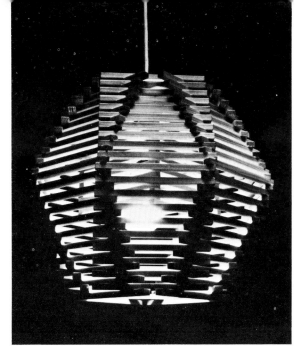

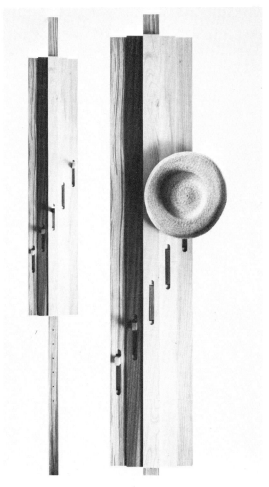

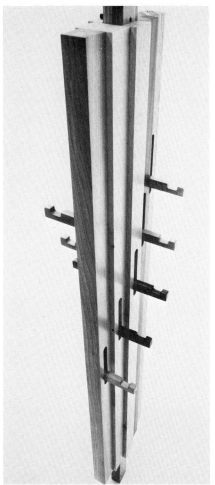

A range of finely
crafted boxes,
designed and made by
Desmond Ryan.

MONEY BOX
Accepts 10p and 5p
coins for parking
meters, the captive lid
sliding either way.
Made from padank and
mahogany.

MONEY 'BLOX'
Cut from padank for
storing coins and rolled
notes.

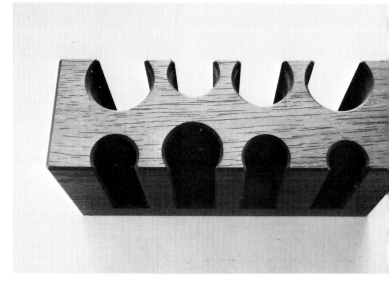

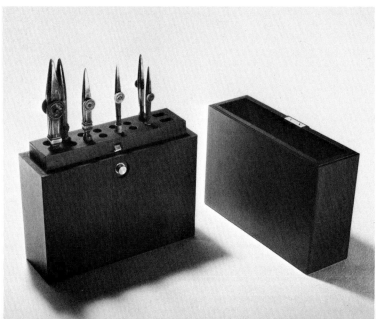

INSTRUMENT BOX
Ebony with brass
fittings.

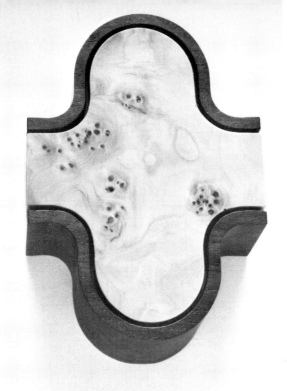

SMALL BOX
Rosewood with yew
lid.

OPERA GLASS BOX
Ebony lined with suede
to house a telescopic
glass.

CUTLERY BOX
Rosewood lined with
suede, the hinge being
of ebony rather than
metal.

JEWELLERY BOX

Three stacking trays in
rosewood with
sycamore dovetails.

Designed and made by
Stephen Hounslow

BOXES

Turned from kingwood.

Designed and made by
David Pye

ICE BUCKET

Turned from ash with
contrasting walnut
laminates and lid
which houses the
tongs.

Designed and made by
Enolinea (Italy)

CONDIMENT SET

Pine with natural or
coloured finish.

Designed and made by
Aarika (Finland)

SALAD BOWL

Turned from teak with oiled finish.

Designed by John Packard (USA) and made by Lumos & Co. Ltd

FRUIT BOWL

Large diameter bowl turned from makamong.

Designed and made by Alan Peters

TRAY

Laminated rosewood
for lightness and
strength.

Made by Tony
McMullen for Robert
Welch Studio Shop

SERVING TRAY

Carved from teak with
oiled finish.

Designed by John
Packard (USA) and
made by Lumos & Co.
Ltd

DISH

Carved from wild
service tree.

Designed and made by
David Pye

17

SMALL SCOOPS
Turned from celery top pine.
Designed and made by Richard Raffan

LEMON SQUEEZER
Turned beech with natural finish.
Designed and made by Casino Designs Ltd

SALAD SERVERS
Carved in teak.
Designed by John Packard (USA) and made by Lumos & Co. Ltd

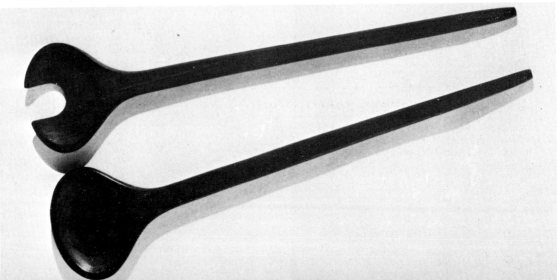

Toys and Recreational Equipment

LETTER BLOCKS

Dovetailing beech blocks.

Designed and made by Paul and Marjorie Abbatt Toys

◁ **HOUSE-GYM AND SLIDE**

Folding beech frame, adjustable platforms and slide with laminate safety surface.

Designed and made by Society of Bros Inc. (USA)

RAINBOW BLOCKS

Beech cubes which assemble in varying colour combinations.

Designed and made by John Adams Toys Ltd

BUILDING BLOCKS AND VEHICLES

Contrasting hardwood blocks and beech chassis.

Designed and made by Willi Müller (Switzerland)

BUILDING BLOCKS

Beech bricks which produce numerous designs.

Designed by Good-Wood Playthings Ltd for Mothercare Ltd

PEG BLOCK

Softwood block with holes and tunnel for the coloured pegs.

Designed by Audrey Stephenson for Paul and Marjorie Abbatt Toys

SEQUENCE BLOCKS

Softwood blocks which assemble in correct sequence.

Designed and made by John Adams Toys Ltd

ROUNDABOUT

Beech with birch ply disc which spirals up and down.

Designed by Susan Wynter and made by Toy Trumpet Workshops Ltd

CATCHING CLOWN

Beech with non-toxic paint finish.

Designed and made by John Adams Toys Ltd

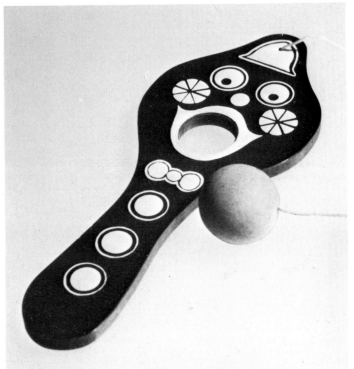

SOMERSAULTING CLOWN

Movement toy with beech ramp and ellipse.

Designed and made by John Adams Toys Ltd

THREADING BOARD

Plywood board with ten holes for varied patterns.

Designed and made by John Adams Toys Ltd

'CATTERPULLER'

Contrasting hardwood sections and wheels glued eccentrically on nylon axles.

Designed and made by Camphill Products

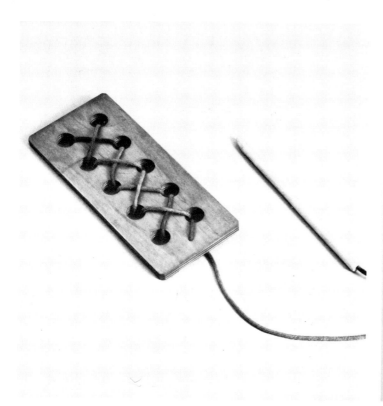

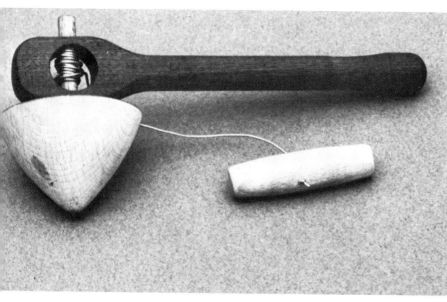

SPINNING TOP

Beech top with metal point.

Designed and made by Astu Studios Ltd

BATH BOAT

White pine finished in waterproof polyurethane.

Designed by David Lethbridge and made by D. L. Playthings Ltd

PADDLE BOAT

Pine and plywood construction, finished in marine varnish.

Designed and made by John Adams Toys Ltd

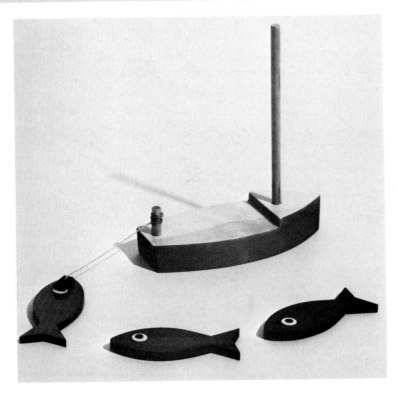

FISHING BOAT

Softwood boat with plasticised magnet to 'hook' fish on deck.

Designed by Panos Athanasskis (Greece) and made by Panos Toys

AEROPLANE

Softwood and ply with
propeller which turns
in the wind.

Designed and made by
Ron Fuller Toys

WARSHIPS

Softwood and ply. The
ship explodes when
button is struck by
torpedo, 'soft' springs
being used and firing
possible only from
horizontal position.

Designed and made by
Ron Fuller Toys

VEHICLES

Birch ply with chunky beech wheels.

Designed by Anthony Kingsley and made by Domat Designs

RACING CAR

Mahogany body and beech wheels.

Designed and made by John Kirk and David Checkland

SPORTS CAR

Teak with removable figures.

Designed and made by M. H. and K. Bunn

FIRE ENGINE AND TRACTOR-TRAILER

Beech and beech ply finished in non-toxic paint.

Designed by Rijk Heuff (Netherlands) for John Adams Toys Ltd

TRUCK

Hardwood of dowelled and pegged construction for assembly and dismantling.

Designed and made by John Kirk and David Checkland

ARTICULATED LORRY

Beech and birch ply with moulded plastic cab.

Designed by M. D. Walker and made by Dalescraft Toys

MINI DOLL'S HOUSE
Five slot-together birch ply panels.
Designed and made by John Adams Toys Ltd

DOLL'S HOUSE
Birch ply with removable front showing interior layout.
Designed by John Parker and made by Domat Designs

DOLL'S HOUSE

Georgian town house in birch ply with hinged front and removable roof.

Designed by John Honeychurch and made by Tridias Ltd

DOLL'S FURNITURE

Birch ply and pine.

Designed by John and Jill Honeychurch and made by Tridias Ltd

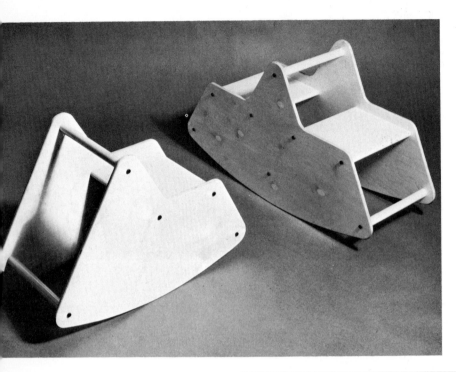

SINGLE AND DOUBLE ROCKERS

Birch ply of knockdown construction.

Designed by Ken Baker and made by Chelsea Furniture Ltd

PLAY EQUIPMENT

Beech units which form varied designs such as a steering wagon and see-saw.

Designed and made by Society of Bros. Inc. (USA)

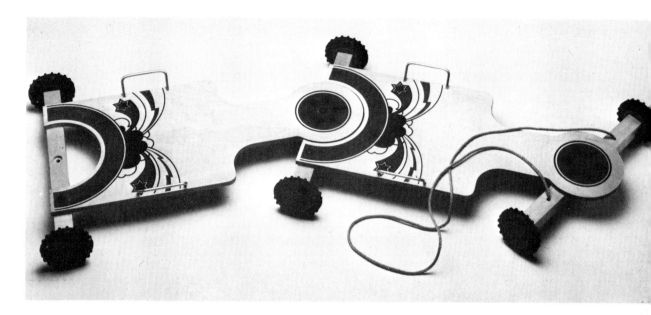

GO-KART
Exterior ply and hardwood axles with detachable rear section.

Designed by John Kirk and David Checkland and made by Scallywag Products

TRICYCLE
Beech and ply with plastic wheels.

Designed and made by James Galt & Co. Ltd

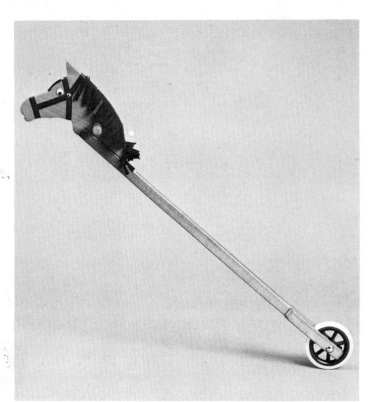

HOBBY HORSE

Beech with leather mane.

Designed by David Lethbridge and made by DL Playthings Ltd

BABY WALKER

A versatile design in beech ply which can be a pram, ride-on toy or toy box.

Designed by Jill Cooper and made by Beaver Toys

ROCKING HORSE

Natural chestnut and
stained elm.

Designed and made by
David Severn

ROCKING HORSE

Douglas fir and hide
saddlery.

Designed and made by
Peter Walmsley

33

TABLE EASEL

Adjustable beech frame for drawing board or artist's canvas.

Designed and made by Winsor and Newton Ltd

WOODWORK BENCH

Of stow-away construction in beech, permits work to be approached from all angles.

Designed and made by Lervad

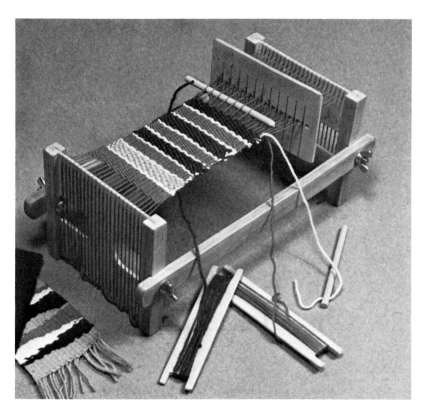

'FIRST LOOM'
Softwood and ply.
Designed and made by
John Adams Toys Ltd

SPINNING WHEEL
New Zealand silver
beech.
Made in New Zealand
for Frank Herring &
Sons

**SKITTLES AND
BALANCING MAN**

Turned from ash with
steel weights.

Designed and made by
Peter Walmsley

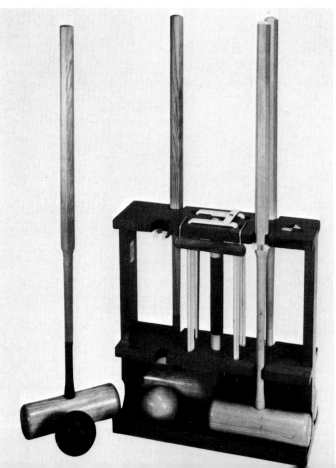

CROQUET SET

Ash mallets and nylon-
coated steel hoops on
beech stand.

Designed and made by
Charles B. Griffith

STOOL

Long stool in acacia.
Designed and made by Alan Peters

◁ EASY CHAIR

Shaped and laminated beech halves slotted together.

Designed by Jens Nielson (Denmark) and marketed by Allard & Co. Ltd

STOOLS

Incorporating jigsaw joints cut from solid yew.

Designed and made by John Makepeace

CHAIR

In olive ash for the interior of a simple chapel.

Designed and made by Alan Peters

STOOL

Carved in cherrywood for twins.

Designed and made by John Makepeace

CHAIR

One of several designs in laminated and bent birch dating back to the 'thirties and still in production.

Designed and made by Alvar Aalto and made by Artek (Finland)

ARMCHAIR

Laminated beech frame and moulded ply.

Designed by Design Lindau & Linderkrantz SIR and marketed by Westnofa (London) Ltd

CHAIR

Plank-back design in sycamore.

Designed and made by Robert Williams of Pearl Dot Ltd

CHAIR

Ash with fabric-covered seat.

Designed and made by Team Schweiz (Switzerland)

ARMCHAIR

Pitch pine with fabric-covered seat.

Designed and made by J. L. Møllers Møbelfabrik (Denmark)

CHAIR

Hardwood with metal joints.

Designed by Bruno Rey and made by Dietiker & Co. AG (Switzerland)

41

Six sculptured chairs of Danish origin.

ARMCHAIR

Teak with fabric seat.

Designed by Ole Wanscher and made by Cado

CHAIR

Rosewood with leather-covered upholstery.

Designed and made by J. L. Møllers Møbelfabrik

CHAIR

Teak with woven cord seating.

Designed and made by J. L. Møllers Møbelfabrik

CHAIR

Teak with wool
upholstered seat.

Designed by Arne
Vodder and made by
Cado

ARMCHAIR

Rosewood with leather-
covered seat.

Designed and made by
J. L. Møllers
Møbelfabrik

ARMCHAIR

Rosewood with leather-
covered seat.

Designed and made by
J. L. Møllers
Møbelfabrik

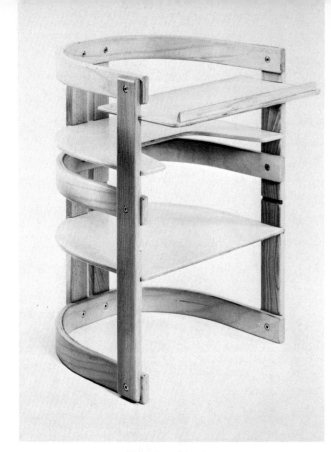

MULTI-PURPOSE CHAIR

Laminated beech construction with adjustable seats and trays. Vertically it functions as baby chair, bar stool or, with two together, cot or desk. Horizontally it becomes bench seat, play frame or, with a plywood head, toy horse.

Designed by Christian Daae-Quale and marketed by Westnofa (London) Ltd

HIGH CHAIR

Beech with splayed legs for stability.

Designed by Ben af Schulten and made by Artek Norrcraft (Finland)

HIGH CHAIR

Birch ply sections which pack flat for travel or storage.

Designed by John Parker and made by Domat Designs.

BAR CHAIR

Laminated beech with vinyl upholstery.

Designed by Ingmar Relling (Norway) and marketed by Westnofa (London) Ltd

ARMCHAIR
Black-stained ash and chromed steel tubes.
Designed and made by Tyson Burrows at Loughborough College of Art and Design

DESK CHAIR
Macassar ebony with finger joints and buffalo suede upholstery.
Designed and made by John Makepeace

ARMCHAIR
Maple with seat and adjustable back of woven maple, treated with wax to prevent noise.
Designed by Poul Kjaeholm and made by E. Kold Christensen A/S (Denmark)

ARMCHAIR

Folding ash frame.

Designed and made by
Linda Shaw at
Loughborough College
of Art and design

SETTEE

Ash frame with leather
armrests and canvas
upholstery.

Designed by Arne
Vodder and made by
Cado (Denmark)

ARMCHAIR

Beech frame with foam
cushions on rubber
webbing and ply back.

Designed by Roland
Gibbard and made by
Design Furniture Group

Chairs by Ernest Gimson dating back to late Victorian times yet still manufactured today by Neville Neal and growing in popularity.

ROCKING CHAIR
Coppice-grown ash poles with dark ebony finish and rush seating.

ARMCHAIR
A finely proportioned version of the traditional ladderback chair in coppice ash with rush seating.

The designs of Lucian R. Ercolani made by Ercol Furniture Ltd are based upon the Windsor chair and combine strength and lightness.

ROCKING CHAIR
Beech frame and elm seat with detachable cushion.

EASY CHAIR
Beech frame with foam cushions on rubber suspension.

ARMCHAIR

Alvar Aalto's cantilever design dating back to 1935 exploits the natural spring of laminated Finnish birch and is the forerunner of many contemporary designs.

Manufactured by Artek (Finland)

EASY CHAIR

Laminated beech frame and lace-on leather cushions over canvas.

Designed by Ingmar Relling (Norway) and marketed by Westnofa (London) Ltd

SWIVEL CHAIR AND STOOL

Bent walnut frames and leather upholstery.

Designed by Martin Grierson and made by Strassle Sohn & Co.

CHAIR AND STOOL

Laminated Finnish birch frames of knock-down construction with canvas upholstery.

Designed by Esko Pajamies and made by Asko-Upo Oy (Finland)

SOFA GROUP

Pine frames of knock-down construction with fabric cushions.

Designed and made by Laukaan Puu Oy (Finland)

SOFA GROUP

Birch knock-down frames with fabric-covered foam cushions. The sofa converts into a double bed.

Designed and made by Kalusto-Kolmio (Finland)

OCCASIONAL TABLE

Glass top on pedestals of mahogany and Indian laurel.

Designed and made by Martin Grierson

◁ DINING TABLE

Black oak with sycamore inlay.

Designed and made by David Field

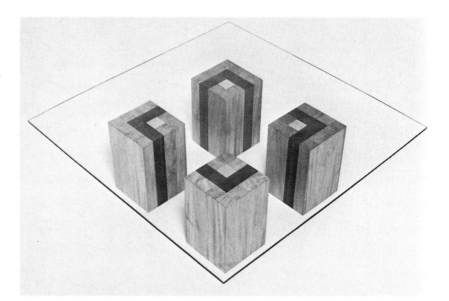

OCCASIONAL TABLE

Hardwood frame and veneered top lacquered white and black.

Designed by Tobia Scarpa and made by Form International

OCCASIONAL TABLE

Bronze glass top on rosewood veneered base with castors.

Designed by Richard Carruthers and made by Merrow Associates

LOW TABLE

Burr walnut with
boxwood inlay.

Designed and made by
David Field

OCCASIONAL TABLE

Burr walnut veneered
top on brass legs.

Designed and made by
Zevi

LOW TABLE

Rosewood with brass
inlay.

Designed and made by
David Field

EXTENSIBLE TABLE

In mahogany with top extending from a circular shape.

Designed and made by Koni Ochsner (Switzerland)

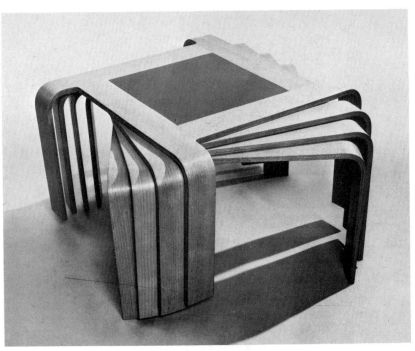

NEST OF TABLES

Moulded laminated ash and melamine.

Designed and made by Jake King at Loughborough College of Art and Design

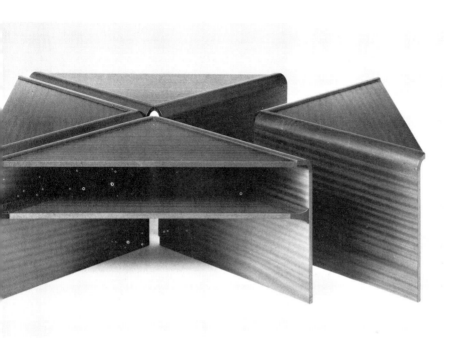

NEST OF TABLES

Four triangular shapes
in veneered and solid
mahogany.

Designed and made by
Koni Ochsner
(Switzerland)

CHESS TABLE

Rosewood with burr
yew inserts. The board
removes in two halves
for access to a suede-
lined storage box.

Designed and made by
Desmond Ryan

GATE-LEG TABLE
American black walnut and African curl mahogany.
Designed and made by Martin Grierson

DINING TABLE
Rosewood veneers and solids, extending from a circle.
Designed by Robert Heritage and made by Heal Furniture Ltd

CONFERENCE TABLE

American black walnut
veneers and solids with
contrasting aluminium
inlay.

Designed by Jens
Risom (USA) and made
by Everest (Long
Eaton) Ltd

DINING TABLE

Rosewood veneers and
solids incorporating
drawers within the top.

Designed by Archie
Shine and made by
Heal Furniture Ltd

TRESTLE TABLE

A folding design in solid ash.

Designed and made by David Field

Constructional details of trestle table showing green acrylic inlay.

TABLE

Oak or ash with finger-joint construction.

Designed by Grahame Amey and David David and made by Grahame Amey Ltd

WALL-MOUNTED TABLE

A folding design with storage shelves in solid and veneered maple.

Designed by Giovanni Ausenda and Guidobaldo Grossi (Italy) and made by Ny Form

EXTENSIBLE TABLE

Ash veneered top which folds in half and swivels over steel frame.

Designed by Guido Pietropoli (Italy) and made by Appiani Selezione

TROLLEY

Afrormosia with heat- and moisture-resistant laminate trays.

Designed by George Ingham and made by Pedley Woodwork Ltd

TROLLEY

Beech frame and teak veneered/green baize top with storage for cards or cutlery underneath.

Designed by Peter Melville and made by East Brothers Ltd

DRINKS TROLLEY

Mahogany veneered and glass construction incorporating storage for glasses and drinks.

Designed and made by Lepofinn (Finland)

TROLLEY

Solid pine construction with glass-topped end-trays.

Designed and made by Enolinea (Italy)

DINING SUITE

Gate-leg table and folding chairs in pine.

Designed and made by
Furniture Factory
Sopenkorpi (Finland)

DINING SUITE

Solid pine with extensible table-top.

Designed and made by
Furniture Factory
Sopenkorpi (Finland)

DINING SUITE

Laminated birch frames
of knock-down
construction with
canvas upholstery.

Designed by Esko
Pajamies and made by
Asko Furniture Division
(Finland)

DINING SUITE

Solid and veneered
maple with fabric
upholstery.

Designed by Giovanni
Ausenda and
Guidobaldo Grosso
and made by Ny Form
(Italy)

**REFECTORY TABLE
AND BENCHES**

Solid pine with pegged
tenon construction.

Designed and made by
Hamlet Furniture Ltd

**REFECTORY TABLE
AND CHAIRS**

Solid and laminated
ash with canvas
seating.

Designed and made by
Cado Furniture (UK)
Ltd

**REFECTORY TABLE
AND BENCHES**

Solid pine construction
with matching chair.

Designed and made by
Furniture Factory
Sopenkorpi (Finland)

STORAGE UNIT
Drawers of plied birch with acrylic bases, pivoting on a stainless steel column.

Designed and made by John Makepeace

◁ **CHEST OF DRAWERS**

Rosewood veneered with brass drop ring handles.

Designed by Peter Liley and made by Heal Furniture Ltd

DISPLAY UNIT

An original idea in ply.

Designed and made by Ueli Berger (Switzerland)

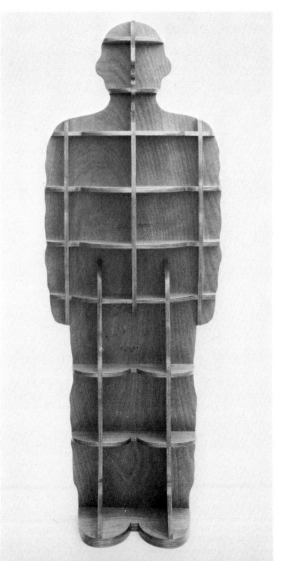

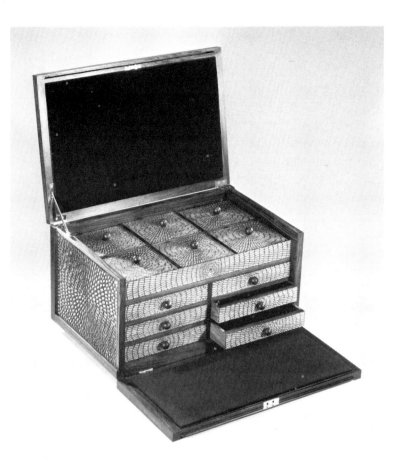

JEWELLERY CHEST

Carved and gilt rosewood with pink silk behind filigree panels and black velvet lining.

Designed and made by Stuart Devlin

STORAGE CABINET

Afrormosia solids and veneers with chromium castors.

Designed by George Ingham and made by Pedley Woodwork Ltd

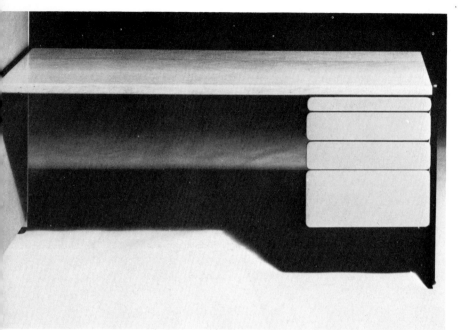

DESK

End-hung construction
with oak veneered top
and PVC painted
drawers.

Designed by P. Cohen,
C. Sykes and S.
Webster and made by
Carson Office Furniture
Ltd

DESK

Oak solids and
veneers.

Designed and made by
Lepofinn (Finland)

DESK

Mahogany solids and veneers with free-standing mobile pedestals.

Designed and made by Pedley Woodwork Ltd

DESK

L-shaped secretarial desk in oak solids and veneers with recessed handles of blued steel.

Designed by Ray Leigh and Trevor Chinn and made by Gordon Russell Ltd

SECRETAIRE

In solid mahogany with
tambour top.

Designed and made by
Hans Eichenberger
(Switzerland)

CABINET BUREAU

Mahogany with
tambour top and front.

Designed and made by
Robert and Trix
Hausman (Switzerland)

72

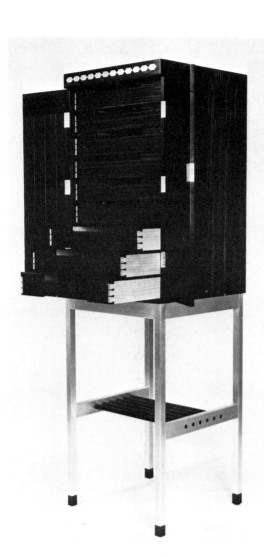

CABINET OF DRAWERS

Macassar ebony with
stainless steel inlay
and aluminium stand.

Designed and made by
Alan Peters

CABINET OF DRAWERS

Rosewood solids and
veneers.

Designed and made by
Kenneth Anderson at
Edinburgh College of
Art

COCKTAIL CABINET

Rosewood veneered finish with glass shelf and chromed steel frame.

Designed by David Falker and made by Merrow Associates Ltd

CABINET

An imaginative construction in solid walnut.

Designed and made by Hans Stöckli and Ibach-Schwyz (Switzerland)

STORAGE CABINET

Rosewood veneers with chromium-plated handles and legs.

Designed by Ray Leigh and Trevor Chinn and made by Gordon Russell Ltd

STORAGE CABINET

Teak solids and veneers on satin chrome legs. The bookcase unit can be mounted separately on legs.

Designed by Abbess Design Group and made by Abbott Bros (Southall) Ltd

SIDEBOARD

Rosewood veneered finish with chromium-plated frame and handles.

Designed by Colin Williams and made by Merrow Associates Ltd

SIDEBOARD

Rosewood veneered carcase on chromium-plated supports – from an integrated range of contract furniture.

Designed by Jan Lunde Knudsen for Infi International Ltd A/S (Norway)

CABINET

Teak solids and
veneers with
chromium-plated
handles and legs.

Designed by Ray Leigh
and made by Gordon
Russell Ltd

TELEPHONE CABINET

Rosewood veneered
finish with pull-out
equipment shelf and
directory trays.

Designed by Ray Leigh
and made by Gordon
Russell Ltd

CORNER CABINET
Solid ash with hand-waxed finish.

Designed and made by Grahame Amey Ltd

CUTLERY CABINET
The oak cabinet holds twelve place settings and lifts from its stand which doubles as a coffee table.

Made by Tony McMullen for Robert Welch Studio Shop

CHEST OF DRAWERS

Solid macrocarpa with drawer handles and sides of mahogany.

Designed and made by Alan Peters

STORAGE CABINET

Oak solids and veneers with recessed handles of blued steel.

Designed by Ray Leigh and Trevor Chinn and made by Gordon Russell Ltd

DRESSING TABLE

White lacquer finished chipboard and ply.

Designed and made by Stag Cabinet Co. Ltd

DRESSING TABLE

In solid sycamore, the side-rests and mirror fold inwards to provide a flat top.

Designed and made by Desmond Ryan

TABLE-BED
Hinged ply units which open out into a bed.

Designed and made by Price Brothers & Co. Ltd

◁STORAGE SYSTEM
Pine-finished panels and plastic connectors. Sliding doors and back panels are available to build storage and room dividers.

Designed and made by Cado

CONVERTIBLE SETTEE
Pine frames with foam cushions on wood springing. With repositioned backrests, single or double beds can be formed.

Designed and made by Price Brothers & Co. Ltd

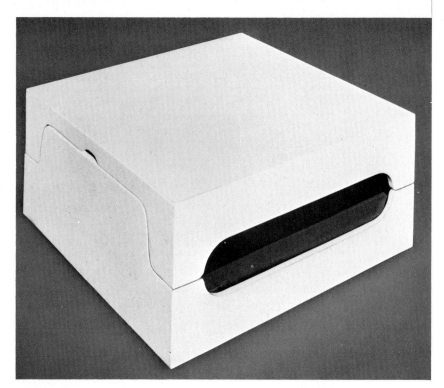

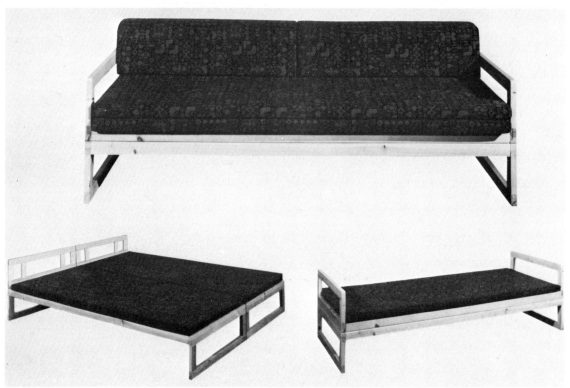

CHAIR

Four square ash frames and polyurethane seat and back. *Right.* The chair in its knock-down form.

Designed by Guiseppe Davanzo and made by Appiani Selezione (Italy)

STOOL

Ply sections and metal joints.

Designed by Kristian Gullichsen and made by Artek Norrcraft (Finland)

STORAGE SYSTEM

Interlocking units of melamine-faced chipboard based on a cube.

Designed by Donald Maxwell and made by Cubestore Ltd

WALL UNITS

Matching drawer, bookcase and corner units finished in natural pine.

Designed and made by Polardesign (Finland)

STORAGE UNITS

Solid and veneered maple components for building shelves and storage units.

Designed by Giovanni Ausenda and Guidobaldi Grossi and made by Ny Form (Italy)

WALL UNITS

Teak-finished cabinets and shelves assembled on free-standing black metal frames.

Designed and made by Avalon Furniture Ltd

STUDY UNITS

Matching lacquered units which can be combined to create work areas for children and students.

Designed by Ahti Taskinen and made by Kalusto-Kolmio (Finland)

CORNER DESK

Supported on four ash frames which can be readily dismantled.

Designed by Guiseppe Davanzo and made by Appiani Selezione (Italy)

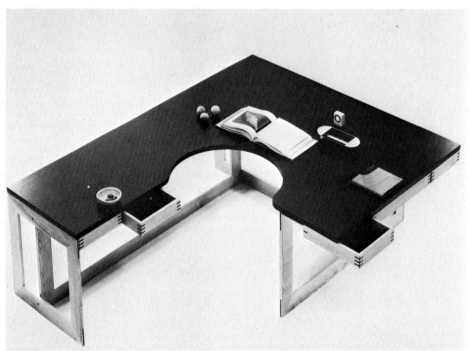

Designed by Jonathan
Morton and made by
H. S. Frazer Ltd

BUNK BED
Ramin frames and
melamine-finished
lockers with castors
and sliding lids.

Designed and made by
Polardesign (Finland)

FITTED BED
Dark-stained mahogany
frames with bedside
units and blanket
boxes providing a
bedhead shelf.

KITCHEN FURNITURE

Interchangeable work and storage units in melamine-faced chipboard.

Designed and made by Hygena Ltd

BATHROOM FURNITURE

A modular system in melamine and PVC faced chipboard which includes vanitory and storage units in addition to bath, shower cubicle, toilet and bidet.

Designed and made by Metlex Industries Ltd